T0130258

Fathers and Sons

Build an Everlasting Relationship

Written and Illustrated By

Miranda Jaye Downing

WestBow Press books may be ordered through booksellers or by contacting:

WestBow Press
A Division of Thomas Nelson & Zondervan
1663 Liberty Drive
Bloomington, IN 47403
www.westbowpress.com
844-714-3454

Because of the dynamic nature of the Internet, any web addresses or links contained in this book may have changed since publication and may no longer be valid. The views expressed in this work are solely those of the author and do not necessarily reflect the views of the publisher, and the publisher hereby disclaims any responsibility for them.

Any people depicted in stock imagery provided by Getty Images are models, and such images are being used for illustrative purposes only. Certain stock imagery © Getty Images.

Interior Image Credit: Miranda Jaye Downing

Scripture quotations are taken from the Holy Bible, New International Version®. NIV®. Copyright © 1973, 1978, 1984 by International Bible Society. Used by permission of Zondervan. All rights reserved.

Scripture quotations are taken from the Holy Bible, New Living Translation, copyright © 1996, 2004, 2015 by Tyndale House Foundation. Used by permission of Tyndale House Publishers Inc., Carol Stream, Illinois 60188. All rights reserved.

Scripture quotations are taken from the Amplified Bible (AMP), Copyright © 2015 by The Lockman Foundation, La Habra, CA 90631. All rights reserved

ISBN: 978-1-6642-8418-0 (sc)
ISBN: 978-1-6642-8417-3 (e)

Library of Congress Control Number: 2022921205

Print information available on the last page.

WestBow Press rev. date: 02/08/2023

WESTBOW
PRESS®
A DIVISION OF THOMAS NELSON
& ZONDERVAN

Check the next page for the hidden messages!

Fathers love their sons.
This one especially loves his boy!
They laugh and play together.
They go for walks and talk about
all kinds of things.

The boy is always learning
things from his father.

Fathers love their sons. This one especially loves his boy! They laugh and play together. They go for walks and talk about all kinds of things.

"But let all who take refuge in you rejoice, let them sing joyful praises forever. Spread your protection over them, that all who love your name may be filled with joy." (Psalms 5:11 NLT)

The boy is always learning things from his father.

"Take my yoke upon you. Let me teach you because I am humble and gentle at heart, and you will find rest for your souls." (Matthew 11:29 NIV)

Fathers teach their boys how to be safe and happy. Sometimes, this means making rules so that people don't get hurt.

Fathers want their boys to feel loved and protected, always!

3

Fathers teach their boys how to be safe and happy. Sometimes, this means making rules so that people don't get hurt.

"Make me walk along the path of your commands for that is where my happiness is found." (Psalms 119:35 NLT)

Fathers want their boys to feel loved and protected, always!

"Joyful are those who obey his laws and search for him with all of their hearts. They do not compromise with evil, and they walk only in his paths." (Psalms 119:2-3 NLT)

Sometimes boys break rules.
Sometimes they are **BIG** rules.
Sometimes they are little rules.

Every time a rule is broken,
someone is hurt or sad.

Sometimes boys break rules.
Sometimes they are **BIG** rules.
Sometimes they are little rules.

"For everyone has sinned;
we all fall short of God's
glorious standard."
(Romans 3:23 NLT)

Every time a rule is broken,
someone is hurt or sad.

"For wherever there
is jealousy and selfish
ambition, there you
will find disorder and
evil of every kind."
(James 3:16 NIV)

6

When the boy breaks a rule, the father puts him in timeout. It is important for him to know that he has made a mistake.

The boy is sad right now because he can't play with his father until timeout is over. Timeout gives him time to think about how breaking rules hurts people.

When the boy breaks a rule, the father puts him in timeout. It is important for him to know that he has made a mistake.

"Because the Lord disciplines those he loves as a father the son he delights in."
(Proverbs 3:12 NIV)

The boy is sad right now because he can't play with his father until timeout is over. Timeout gives him time to think about how breaking rules hurts people.

"When a crime is not punished quickly, people feel it is safe to do wrong."
(Ecclesiastes 8:11 NLT)

The boy's father is sad too.
He hopes the boy learns why
he shouldn't do bad things.

Just because the boy has done
a bad thing, doesn't mean the
father stopped loving him.

9

The boy's father is sad too.
He hopes the boy learns why
he shouldn't do bad things.

"I used to wander off until you
disciplined me, but now I closely
follow your word."
(Psalms 119:67 NLT)

Just because the boy has done
a bad thing, doesn't mean the
father stopped loving him.

"Nothing can separate
us from the love of God."
(Romans 8:39 NIV)

The boy's father wants him to know that he can always ask for help, no matter what.

So, the father sends his other son...

The boy's father wants him to know that he can always ask for help, no matter what.

"The Lord hears his people when they call to him for help. He rescues them from all their troubles." (Psalms 34:17 NLT)

So, the father sends his other son...

"For God so loved the world that he gave his one and only Son, that whoever believes in him shall not perish, but have eternal life." (John 3:16 NIV)

12

As the timer ticks down, the son says,
"I know how you can get out of timeout."

The boy looks up hopefully.

13

Now, close your eyes, and speak from your heart...

As the timer ticks down, the son says, "I know how you can get out of timeout."

The boy looks up hopefully.

"I am the way, the truth and the life. No one can come to the father except through me." (John 14:6 NIV)

"So each generation should set its hope anew in God, not forgetting his glorious miracles, and keeping his commands." (Psalms 78:7 NLT)

Now, close your eyes, and speak from your heart...

14

The son asks, "Do you trust me?"

"Yes."

"Are you sorry?"

"Yes."

The son asks, "Do you trust me?"

"Yes."

"Those who know
your name trust in
you, for you, Lord,
have never forsaken
those who seek you."
(Psalms 9:10 NIV)

"Are you sorry?"

"Yes."

"Repent then, and
turn to God so that your
sins may be wiped out, that
times of refreshing may
come from the Lord."
(Acts 3:19 NIV)

"Great!" the son says. "I forgive you."
It sounds like someone is cheering in the other room!

The boy is so happy, but then he asks,
"Shouldn't Father be the one to forgive
me? It was his rule that I broke..."

"Great!" the son says. "I forgive you."
It sounds like someone is cheering in the other room!

"In the same way, I tell you, there is rejoicing in the presence of the angels of God over one sinner who repents." (Luke 15:10 NIV)

The boy is so happy, but then he asks, "Shouldn't Father be the one to forgive me? It was his rule that I broke..."

"The Pharisees and the teachers of religious law said to themselves, 'Who does he think he is? That's blasphemy! Only God can forgive sins!'" (Luke 5:21 NLT)

18

"I know," the son replied. "But he said it was okay. In fact, he said you could only go back to him once you and I talked."

The son smiled at the boy. "Now, go to him," he said. "He misses you."

"I know," the son replied. "But he said it was okay. In fact, he said you could only go back to him once you and I talked."

"'But I want you to know that the Son of Man has authority on earth to forgive sins.' So he said to the paralyzed man, 'I tell you, get up, take your mat and go home.'" (Luke 5:24-25 NIV)

The son smiled at the boy. "Now, go to him," he said. "He misses you."

I have swept away your offences like a cloud, your sins like the morning mist. Return to me for I have redeemed you." (Isaiah 44:22 NIV)

The boy's father is so happy to have his son back! The boy learned that if he was sorry for his mistakes, loved his father and brother, and tried to do the right thing, he wouldn't to have to stay in timeout.

"Whoever conceals their sins does not prosper, but the one who confesses and renounces them finds mercy." (Proverbs 28:13 NIV)

In fact, the boy decided that if he had another brother or sister in timeout, he would tell them how to get out too!

"And then he told them, go into all the world and preach the good news to everyone." (Mark 16:15 NLT)

You, reader, are God's son, God's daughter.
Go to Him, He misses you.

"So he got up and went to his father. But while he was still a long way off, his father saw him and was filled with compassion for him; he ran to his son, threw his arms around him and kissed him."

Luke 15:20 NIV (The Parable of the Lost Son)

References
Bible: New International Version (NIV)
Bible: New Language Translation (NLT)

A special thank you to my husband, Josh, for his spiritual, fundamental, and practical support. All of this started with you "spreading the Good News."

Thank you, family and friends, for your support and encouragement along the way.

And for my boys, each one a wonderful blessing and a constant reminder of God`s perfect love, grace, and mercy.

God loves His children, and we are all His children. If you're wanting to know what that love feels like, open your heart to Him, say:

"Father, I want to know your love.
I believe you sent your Son, Jesus,
to die on the cross and rise again
to wipe away my sins. Jesus,
I make you my Lord, my Savior.
Amen"

Printed in the United States
by Baker & Taylor Publisher Services